Get Better!

Smart Business Advice From Unexpected Mentors

KEN OKEL

I0427404

ISBN: 9798879232547
ISBN-13: 979-8-8792325-4-7

DEDICATION

None of us *Get Better* without the help and support of others. Thank you to all who have offered me words of encouragement.

It's my hope that I will continue your legacy and contribute in the same way to others.

TABLE OF CONTENTS

Introduction   7

Katie the Custodian   13

The Dennis Decision   25

Amanda the Author   33

20 Pushups Pat   39

Frustration Is a Choice   47

Get To Tomorrow   55

Beautiful Is Hard   71

Don't Open the Oven   79

Watch Yourself Willie   87

Don't Be Afraid   93

The Uninspiring Examples   99

About the Author   109

Bulk Orders of This Book   112

INTRODUCTION

I remember the day when I grew tired of billionaire success stories. Please understand that I often find tales of super successful people and mega-corporations to be interesting and inspiring.

But, in most cases, while I admire them all, I can't relate to them in my everyday life. In these stories, success is usually tied to some kind of unique advantage or simply being in the right place at the right time.

There's nothing relatable or repeatable about their success recipe, other than perhaps a catchy slogan or a simplistic solution. It's unattainable good fortune.

Today's Workplace

I know a lot of people who are struggling at work. They are searching for actionable advice, as their days are full of unexpected change, new demands, doing more with less, and endless requests to innovate.

Meanwhile, they feel increasingly disconnected from their workplace culture. They like the kind of work that they do but are starving for motivation and encouragement.

I also know some leaders are struggling with their pep talks. Simply saying, "You'll be fine," as someone has to do the work of two positions, is not effective.

And saying an extremely successful person told you to "Reach for the stars," or "Turn your first million into five million," doesn't help and quickly becomes a turnoff.

These professionals find themselves in a radically different workplace. They can sense that something is just off with their work world. But they don't know what to do to improve and there seems to be no end to their suffering.

The Idea

I started thinking about the times when a few words of advice were game-changing for me. I realized that some of the best advice I've ever received came from ordinary moments, from everyday people.

None of them have climbed mountains, scored Super Bowl touchdowns, or created mega companies. But while their bank accounts may not have million or billion dollar balances, each one offered me something priceless and memorable.

This book is full of those stories. Granted, it is not a magic wand for every workplace problem. But it's a start.

You're going to meet some very interesting people who approach their lives and jobs differently. Their lessons can improve our lives.

Where did I meet them? I've collected their stories during my time spent in broadcast news, hurricane relief, and even professional ballet. And today, as a motivational keynote speaker, I've added to the collection, as my presentations give me a great opportunity to meet interesting people offstage.

Some of the popular stories I share with audiences see me reenact being attacked by a police dog (while wearing a padded suit) or using a ballet move to demonstrate the concept of trust. These are physical and visual lessons that I love to share but understand they don't have the same impact on the printed page, so you won't find them in this book. But if you need a keynote for your next event...

The stories in this book are perfect in chapter form. In some cases, I'm able to add some extra elements that don't fit when I'm telling them on stage.

A Book for the Busy

This book was written with a busy professional in mind. Let's face it, who doesn't have a growing to-do list and not enough hours in the day?

As with my previous book, *Stuck On Yellow*, you can read the chapters in any order. Some chose to read a chapter a day and make the book part of their daily or weekly ritual. Others assign chapters to their teams and discuss the lessons at staff meetings.

I also like how these stories are my discoveries and are new to you. They won't come up in a Google search. At least not yet! They come from personal interactions.

And while there's power in a good story, I felt this book also needed some kind of next step or action plan. Empowerment begins with memorable and actionable advice.

In this book, you'll get a combo plate of advice. Each chapter will highlight a specific story. Then we'll cover the big picture takeaways. Finally, you'll be empowered with next steps or important questions that you might want to ask yourself or your team.

I throw a curveball in the final chapter. That one highlights some real examples of bad behavior or habits that you want to avoid. While I tried to give this book a very positive tone, there are some lessons to be learned from those who come up short.

Before You Ask

People want to know, "Are these stories real?" The people are real and the things that happened are like they happened. Names and certain details have been changed to protect privacy.

Pay attention to what's happening around you, as you might be missing some great stories. When the events in this book took place, there were no trumpets sounding, letting me know something important was occurring.

Fortunately, I'm good at taking notes and remembering a random thing that might have some value down the road.

Enjoy the stories. Grow and get better from the advice.

KATIE THE CUSTODIAN

This story begins on the 17th floor of a downtown office building. I'm visiting a high-powered law firm.

At the time, I was conducting a training session with some of the firm's attorneys, helping them improve their presentation skills.

The training was happening after hours and eventually it was time for me to go home. This would see me leave the conference room, walk through the firm's impressive glass entrance, and then take the elevator to the parking deck.

The office was quiet as I walked toward the imposing glass double doors. This was an entrance that sent a clear message of power and authority. I have no idea what the firm's billable hour rate was but the entrance sent a signal that if money was an issue, you probably should not come inside.

But on that day, I wasn't able to exit because my path was blocked. A woman was standing in front of the glass doors. She was facing the doors, with her back to me.

The woman is wearing jeans, a polo shirt, and she's holding a rag in her right hand. She's motionless, as she stares, like she's in a trance, at the glass doors.

I want to go home but I don't want to scare her. I do the thing where you shuffle your feet and clear your throat, hoping to get her out of her trance.

I succeed and she jumps a little, steps back, and says, "I'm so sorry sir. I was looking for smudges."

That's when I noticed the cart, off to the side. The custodian's cart. I had just met *Katie the Custodian*.

I smile and start to pass through the double doors. But as I do so, I slow down and playful inspect them.

"It looks pretty clean to me," I say.

Katie responds by saying, "It does but I'll be back tomorrow."

A few months later, I returned to the law firm for another employee training session. During a break, I started chatting with the managing partner, otherwise known as the boss of the law firm. Before long, I brought up Katie.

"I have to tell you, your custodian is really dedicated when it comes to cleaning," I said.

The managing partner laughed and said, "You know Katie probably has more job security than anyone else in this office, including me."

Then I found out what set Katie apart.

A Different Approach

Over the years, the firm had a series of custodians. Most were okay but never memorable.

They saw their job as simply cleaning up the mess. You'd vacuum the office, pick up the trash, and clean the restrooms. The office is restored to its previous condition.

Katie took a different approach to her job. She wanted to make sure things in the firm never got too dirty. And this led her to perform her work in some different ways, as she was always looking for smudges.

First, she studied the office and looked at problem areas, the places that always seemed to get messy. Then she figured out the root cause of the situation.

For instance, at the firm, high-value client lunches were a big deal. The luxurious conference room would host these events, which were part work, part lunch, and all about keeping the business relationship strong.

These lunches were well orchestrated affairs, where paying attention to little details was important. However, even the most planned sessions could be undermined by an unintended negative impression.

While the conference room had an impressive table, comfortable chairs, and a great view, it also featured trash cans that were smaller than a shoebox.

This created problems because the lunches produced a certain amount of boxes, wrappers, and leftovers. While the food was great, the room would end up looking messy.

Katie realized there was a problem with these important events. She was always looking for smudges, so on her own, she took action.

Whenever she learned of a client lunch, she would bring in a few larger trash cans. When the group took a break, she would swoop in, clear out the trash, and tidy up the room.

Just these strategic adjustments made the lunches feel more professional. People noticed.

The Copy Room

Katie would look for smudges in unexpected places. Like the firm's copy room, which can get quite a daily workout.

She studied the room and realized the flow was wrong. It was too easy for paper to end up on the floor or things like pens and other office supplies, intended for that space, to disappear.

The room had been an ongoing source of frustration for employees. But like many problems at work, people had become accustomed to them and didn't think a solution was possible. Katie decided to do something about it.

The custodian rearranged the recycling and shredding bins to ensure paper ended up in the right place and not on the floor. Katie made stencils of the room's office supplies, so every item had an identified home, making it harder for someone to accidentally walk off with it.

Before long, the room is cleaner and a more effective space.

The Culture Transformation

Over time, all of these changes made the office cleaner than it had been in years. People noticed and before long, some old and messy habits started to change.

The firm's managing partner was known for drinking five Diet Cokes a day. As he traveled from meeting to meeting, he would leave behind countless water rings on desks and tables.

But the managing partner respected and appreciated the work Katie performed and decided he didn't want to add to her workload.

For the first time ever, he started to use coasters. And with him setting an example, others started to change their behaviors. They saw how a clean office made it a better place to work. No one wanted to undermine Katie's legacy.

In a high-powered business environment, *Katie the Custodian* was likely one of the firm's lowest paid employees. And yet, she had a tremendous impact on employee culture. That was Katie, looking for smudges.

And while her colleagues were some of the best orators you'll ever meet, she wasn't known for her words. As a shy person, she kept conversations short and to the point.

Katie talked through her actions, more than her words. And while making eye contact could make her feel uncomfortable, she had no fear when it came to staring down a mess. For her, it was a problem that needed to be solved.

But Wait, There's More

About two years later, this story took an unexpected turn and got a new ending. I was back at the law firm, training a new group of associates in presentation skills. During a break, I found the managing partner and I mentioned how audiences had been enjoying the story of *Katie the Custodian*. I asked how Katie was doing.

"She left about six months ago," he said sadly. "Her family had a great opportunity on the other side of the country and they decided to move. We held a big goodbye party for her. Don't worry, we didn't make her clean up afterward."

I was stunned but from everything I saw, the law firm continued to look spotless.

"Looks like you must have hired another great custodian," I said.

"We love *Karl the Custodian*," he said with a smile. "But Katie played a big part in his success. Remember how she was always looking for smudges? That's how she handled her departure."

I found out that as soon as Katie gave her two weeks' notice, she started taking notes on a legal pad, as she did her job. She wrote down how she cleaned, what products she used, and who were the people and places that needed a little extra attention.

All of this cleaning information was left with the office manager. By the time Karl started cleaning, he had a roadmap. He didn't have to guess how the firm wanted things to be done.

Big Picture Takeaways

We love employees who are self-motivated and will look for better ways to do things. *Katie the Custodian* is a great example of how innovation and improvement can come from any level of an organization.

Katie was allowed a certain amount of freedom in her job, as long as she fulfilled the basic responsibilities. She didn't have an office full of people telling her how to clean. And in this case, the legal professionals probably could not afford to be overly involved in cleaning rituals.

In many cases, leaders must nurture innovation. If you're not careful, employees may believe their contributions are limited by their job descriptions.

It's important to figure out what's the right balance between following the rules or questioning them. Very often, tomorrow's innovators are today's rebels. Will you embrace them or push them away?

Your actions are seen by all and if you're regarded as someone who shoots down new ideas, then the members of your team may hold their tongues the next time inspiration strikes.

Action Steps

If you want to have an organization that is full of new ideas, then you must let it be known through visible actions.

Set aside time for people to pitch new ideas. Then give yourself a chance to review them.

You don't have to follow any of the new ideas but simply having a way to share and discuss potential best practices can enrich your workplace culture. Your employees will know they were heard.

People will also need time to discover new things. This might involve attending conferences, reading articles, or networking with colleagues. Doing the same activities, through business as usual, will likely not produce brilliance.

While there are no guarantees a commitment to innovation will result in breakthroughs, what will you gain if people's knowledge grows more and more out of date?

Create a work culture where employees are encouraged to show thought leadership, no matter their position.

When expectations are set high, your employees will often grow to meet them.

THE DENNIS DECISION

A chance meeting at a manufacturing trade show taught me an important lesson about the big decisions we make in our lives. And the takeaways are especially important for business owners to consider.

The person at the center of this story is Dennis. I met him while walking the show floor, which is something I like to do when I'm speaking to members of an industry that is new to me. I was dazzled by the massive machines that were on display.

At these kinds of events, when I walk by a company booth, I'm often approached enthusiastically by sales representatives. But when they look closely at my name badge and see the words, "Keynote Speaker," they tend to quickly lose interest in me and disappear. I understand, as there's no chance I'm in the market to buy a machine that's a tight squeeze in a semi-trailer truck.

But Dennis was different. He was happy to talk to a stranger, with no buying authority, about his company. During our chat, Dennis spoke with passion about the product and boiled it down into simple terms.

Later, he told me this month was a special one for him.

"I've been with this company for 30 years," Dennis said proudly.

As a former journalist, when I hear a statement like this, I get curious. As a speaker and an author, I think there might be a good story to tell.

I asked Dennis, "How did you end up at this company? Often, when someone is in a place for decades, they're part of a family business or were there when the firm started. But it doesn't sound like you fit in either of those groups."

"It all began 30 years ago, when I was honorably discharged from the Navy," he said. "I needed to find a job and I figured my skill set matched up well with manufacturing."

The Strategy

I found out that, although Dennis knew where he wanted to live, he didn't know which manufacturing business would be the best fit for his civilian life.

"Back then there was no Google," Dennis said. "It was harder to find out which were the best companies."

Eventually, he came up with a creative strategy that would allow him to quickly evaluate the marketplace. It would take a day to accomplish.

"In the morning, I got in my car with a big bottle of Fanta Root Beer," he said. "Then I drove to eight nearby manufacturers."

"Did you go inside each place and check things out?" I asked.

"No, I never got out of the car," Dennis said with a smile. "I'd pull up, look around, take a couple of sips of root beer, and then go to the next place."

"No applications, meetings, or conversations with current employees?" I said.

"Nope, just a map of the city, some root beer, and my eyes," he said. "By the end of the day, I knew where I wanted to work. There was no doubt."

"How did you decide?" I asked. "Was it just a hunch or a lucky guess?"

"I looked at the employee parking lot at each company," Dennis said. "I figured the place that had the best cars or the nicest cars was probably one that paid well. And really good cars in the employee parking lot were probably a sign of a successful business."

Imagine Dennis making a 30-year decision based on what he saw in a parking lot. For him, it was the right call.

Big Picture Takeaways

In your business, consider that potential employees and customers may judge you based on factors you've never considered. Dennis was looking for signs that success filtered down to the workforce. He found them in the parking lot.

You may have spent a tremendous amount of time on marketing and branding but people may evaluate you on something random. You can't control what their eyes see.

Note that I said random but not out of your control. That's why I tell people to consider the first impression your business makes on customers.

If they pull up to a physical location, what do they see? Does your parking lot look like a place where old fast food bags go to die? That makes an impression.

If you have an automated phone system, does it contain out-of-date information or require customers to navigate through an endless and confusing series of menus?

Let's say you run an air conditioning repair company. You may have the greatest repair technicians but when someone calls customer service, to set up an appointment, do they encounter someone who is rude or indifferent? Does that attitude convince the customer to take their business elsewhere?

Beware of lasting impressions, left to chance.

Action Steps

In today's world, looking at the quality of cars in the employee parking lot may not be the best strategy for finding a new job. But periodically consider the intangibles that could be limiting your hiring or customer acquisition processes.

Not sure what they might be? Then you might want to hire some mystery shoppers to give you an outside perspective. Others will enlist the help of focus groups.

Talk to employees about these things and make them understand how these issues can become barriers to success.

Finally, Dennis was a good ambassador for his company, even with someone who would never be a customer. Can all of your employees (and I mean all of them) speak with authority about your business to a stranger? If not, schedule some training sessions.

Embrace the random observation. Great words of wisdom can come from anywhere.

AMANDA THE AUTHOR

An author, who wrote a book I had no intention of ever reading, taught me a valuable lesson about making a commitment to a goal.

At the time, I was attending a program at my local library, where published authors are interviewed about their books. I enjoy these events because they give you a chance to learn more about what went into the writing of the books, as well as the authors.

While the biography on the dust jacket gives you a portrait of the writer, it really doesn't give you a feel for the total person. And perhaps it makes them seem too perfect.

Writing a book is hard and getting it edited and published is even more challenging. I have a lot of respect for every author.

If I'm not speaking on the road, I'll almost always try to attend these sessions, as I find them informative and creatively inspiring.

You might be surprised to learn, that in most cases, I haven't read the book that's being discussed. It's usually for one of three reasons:

1. While I love to read, I'm a slow reader who doesn't have a tremendous amount of time to read.

2. I'll use the presentation as a way to evaluate the author. If the author seems interesting, then I might pick up the book.

3. There are some great books that just are not for me.

In this case, it was the third reason. Amanda had written an award-winning book that was aimed at a female audience. It's just not my cup of tea. If one day it's made into a movie, then I might check it out.

I was impressed when Amanda told the audience how she came up with her story, fleshed out the characters, and tapped into themes that audience members said made them think about the novel, long after they finished it.

At the end of each session, there's a short question and answer period. As a former journalist, I'm not shy about raising my hand.

"Can you tell us about how you wrote your book? What's your writing process?" I asked.

I'm always curious about the answer to this behind the scenes query. I've learned some authors write a book during a short period of time, while a few write it for years.

Others will book a hotel room for a couple of weeks and write the book in total isolation from their everyday lives. A few will go to an everyday location, like a coffee shop, at a set time every day.

And some successful writers are driven by the publishing calendar. They know that if they hope to have a book published every year, they need to meet certain deadlines. No new book, no new money.

In any case, the answer exposes a different side of the author than is portrayed on the book jacket.

Amanda laughed at my question and then surprised everyone with her answer.

"I have three young kids and a full-time job, so I don't have a lot of time to write," she said. "Every day, I wake up two hours early to write. My house is quiet at 5 a.m. and I can concentrate."

I asked, "Do you write in a special place?"

"I sit on the floor of my bedroom closet and write on my laptop," she responded.

Amanda's answer shows a special dedication

to her craft.

"If I go somewhere else in my home, that will likely wake someone up. The closet is quiet and I won't be interrupted," she said. "It's really the only chance I'll have to write all day."

While her writing space is non-traditional, it works for her, and she was using it again while writing her second novel.

Big Picture Takeaways

How many of us have a goal but don't have the commitment to see it through? Think back to your New Year's resolutions or some personal milestone you wanted to achieve. Did you make it happen or was it an unrealized dream?

Amanda has a very busy life and it would be understandable if she postponed writing her first novel.

But she found a way to make it happen. Amanda decided she would sacrifice sleep and comfort. In exchange, the story that had been in mind for years became a reality.

Action Steps

Think about your goals and dreams. How will you manifest them?

What's the variable that's holding you back? Is it something like time or money? You might remove it as a barrier through some reallocation.

Take your goal and come up with a roadmap for how you can achieve it. You may also want to share it with family and friends, so you'll earn their support.

This discussion may lead to your finding an accountability partner. While this person may not share your goal, they should have a goal of their own. That way you can support each other on your journeys.

It's easy to see the success of the moment and not recognize the challenges that were overcome.

20 PUSHUPS PAT

During my news reporting days, the search for a story led me to an important lesson in tough love. At the time, I had a front row seat to see the power of nature, as a flood threatened large parts of Southern Illinois.

The waters of the Ohio River kept rising and that saw homeowners evacuating to higher ground. Those who waited too long found escape routes flooded over. And some cars became inoperable as high waters flooded engines and stalled plans.

A few stayed and fought the waters,

surrounding their homes with countless sandbags. Others accepted the fact their homes would be flooded and moved their most valuable possessions to the second floor.

The Reporting Challenge

When you're sent to cover a natural disaster, you don't have a set story. You may have an idea of what you could cover. But there are several factors you have to keep in mind:

1. Can you reach where the action is taking place? This might see you abandon your news car, near high waters you can't drive through, and hitch a ride on a passing tractor. Later, you'll worry about how you'll get back to your car and ultimately file your report.

2. You need to keep your eyes open for something dramatic and unexpected that may happen. This could replace your original story and you'll have to explain to the station why you're making the switch.

3. As a news crew, you'll likely be tired, uncomfortable, and hungry for some of

the day. That's part of the job. You have to remember your suffering is nothing compared to those who are living through the disaster. Also, focus your stories on people and their challenges and not just government officials and statistics.

The Discovery

On the fifth day of covering the flood, my photographer and I were driving through a small town, looking for something new to share with viewers, when we saw a huge mound of sand that had been dumped in a park.

We pulled over and found a story. And that's when we met Pat.

Pat was a corrections officer from a nearby juvenile detention center. While he was near retirement age, he didn't remind me of a kindly grandfather. Pat looked tough and you immediately recognized his authority.

On that day, he was in charge of a work crew of about 20 young men from the detention center. They had been brought in as extra help to fight the flood.

All the young men had committed some kind of crime. Now they were attacking the sand with shovels and burlap bags. They worked in teams, scooping up the sand, and then putting it into the bags. It's physical, hard work.

"We're filling hundreds of sandbags today," Pat told us. "They'll be used to protect homes and businesses. People will use them to build a barrier against the rising waters."

Pat told me that while the work was demanding, the inmates welcomed it as it was a chance to be outside and enjoy a break in their daily routine.

We started to get video of the operation and a short while later Pat stopped the group.

"Gentlemen, take a ten-minute break," Pat ordered. "Put your feet up or run to the restroom. But don't be late coming back."

Almost everyone ran to the nearby park restroom. Roughly nine minutes later, the juvenile detainees started running back and lining up in front of Pat, just like you would see with an Army Drill Sergeant.

All of them arrived before the end of the ten-minute break. But the last one back was given a special order.

"Okay Mickey, give me 20," Pat said to the last one. He was about two seconds slower than the next to last person.

Without complaining, Mickey dropped to the ground, performed 20 pushups, and then returned with everyone else to the sandbagging operation.

Later I asked, "Why did you have Mickey do pushups, when he wasn't late from his break?"

"We have a rule that whenever these kids do something as a group, the last one to finish has to give me 20 pushups," Pat said.

"Even if you're barely last and not late?" I

asked.

"For years, no one has held these kids accountable," Pat said. "Last is last and where they finish is a choice. They need to understand that actions come with consequences."

I learned this applied to many activities, from getting on the transport bus to lining up for a sip of water at a drinking fountain. If you were someone who wasn't very motivated, your day would be full of pushups.

While none of the detainees would likely nominate Pat as employee of the month, I could tell they respected him. There was no arguing. He was tough but fair.

Big Picture Takeaways

In business, there are no detainees. But there are standards which can set you apart from others.

While Pat provided tough love to the detainees, the rules were well-defined. The kids understood what was at stake and their control of the situation.

A thoughtful approach to simple activities can create teachable moments.

Action Steps

Define the standards you want in your business and your life. Do you communicate them to others?

If people don't know your expectations, then it's hard to follow them. They're more likely to guess what you want, and often, the guess is wrong.

For instance, how would you want employees to finish the sentence, "We are the kind of business where people go the extra mile by…"

You don't want people to finish that sentence their way. It needs to be your words, your philosophy.

Also, decide what are the moments when tough love is appropriate. While I'm a big fan of positive feedback, honest feedback may be more valuable at times.

Some leaders fall into the trap of selectively delivering criticism or not doing so across the entire organization. Remember, Pat did not play favorites. Last was last, no matter who finished last.

Finally, if you're a leader, make sure you're following your own standards. It can be tempting to bend the rules but if these moments are seen by others, you may be hurting your work culture.

Don't believe that big lessons have to come in big moments. Well considered, thoughtful actions can have a lasting impact.

FRUSTRATION IS A CHOICE

How do you handle frustration at work? On the job, you may have found yourself the victim of a subjective decision.

You may believe you were the best person for a promotion, to lead a new project, or to attend an important conference. But someone else was selected.

This kind of disappointment can burn inside your mind. Sometimes, those fires of disappointment go out after an hour or two. You accept the decision, even if you don't agree with it.

There are also those cases when the fires of negativity grow in your mind, and you start to resent your job. Your performance goes down. People notice and you fall further down when it comes to future consideration for special opportunities.

How can we channel disappointment in a way that can lead to future growth? I found the answer in the world of professional ballet.

As you may know, I had no dance background when I accepted the position of Executive Director, with the four million dollar business.

I wasn't in charge of teaching people how to dance. Instead, the job was about fundraising, marketing, and keeping the doors open when cash was tight, which turned out to be just about every day.

My background as a reporter came in handy, as I wasn't shy about asking questions that might seem obvious to someone who had spent their life in dance. The answers often supplied me with important things to mention to our supporters. Sometimes they weren't just about dancing.

I received one of these priceless life lessons from Gina the Ballerina. And it was about dealing with frustration at work.

Meet Gina

While all of our dancers were extremely talented, Gina was probably the best female performer. Technically, she was perfect. She knew all the moves.

But what set her apart was her ability to convey emotion through dance. Whether it was a facial expression or how she held her body, if you were in the audience, you knew what Gina's character was feeling.

Remember, in ballet, there's no talking but often there are very dramatic emotions being expressed on stage. Think about the challenge of conveying rage, joy, or envy simply through your movements.

In my mind, the best female dancer should get the best female role in our productions. And that would be Gina.

But that didn't always happen. I was thinking about the ballet selection process, like football, where the best quarterback becomes the starting quarterback.

In the world of ballet, the roles are cast through a more subjective process. The task falls to the choreographer, the composer of the production.

When casting the main female role, the choreographer may favor someone who is taller or shorter than Gina, has some other intangible quality, or most closely resembles the first person who ever danced the part. It's very subjective.

In whatever role she received, Gina would do a great job with the character and would really shine in any solos or duets.

When we put on a major production that ran for several days, I would watch it from different perspectives in the audience. No matter where I sat, Gina always dazzled the crowd in her role, even if it was not the big one.

The Gina Way

After a performance, you'd often find me taking some time to congratulate the dancers. Once, when talking to Gina, I offered the usual compliments. But on that night, it felt like I needed to say something more.

"Gina, you're so good and audiences love your performances. But I've got to ask, do you ever get frustrated when you don't get the lead role?"

Gina responded with four words that changed my perspective. She said, "Frustration is a choice."

"Tell me more because frustration at work is often hard for me to shake," I said.

"As a dancer, my career will only last for so long and there are only so many performances I'll get to do. One day it will end," she said. "Do

I want to spend one of those valuable performances feeling angry or upset? Or do I want to make a better choice?"

Gina admitted that when she was up for a big part, she wanted the role. She's competitive. But she also knew no matter how hard she tried, the outcome was not guaranteed.

For Gina, *Frustration Is a Choice* meant that she was going to focus all her skill and talent, as a dancer, on whatever role she received.

Even if it was a smaller one, she would find a way to make it stand out and be memorable. In those moments, she would make the audience sit up, notice, and feel something.

And it wasn't like she was using her talents to show up the other dancers or make them look bad. While it might be tempting to show off and make the choreographer regret not casting her in a larger role, that wasn't what Gina was about.

She wanted to shine in a way that would elevate the entire performance and not just put a spotlight on herself.

In a world where we often judge ourselves by the size or prominence of our roles, Gina chose to focus on what she could control.

Big Picture Takeaways

We have the ability to channel negative feelings of rejection into something positive. This can become a healthy habit, as a certain amount of disappointment is a part of life and work.

Opportunities to shine are limited. Make the most of the ones you get. It is possible to shine doing something ordinary.

Remember, your behavior in a moment of rejection, will be seen and felt by others. Decide if you want to show them your best and most generous side or become an object of pity.

Action Steps

You'll need self-discipline to embrace the philosophy of *Frustration Is a Choice*. It may be tempting to fall back on old habits and feelings.

Some find it helps to write down their commitment to making the most out of a disappointing outcome.

You might say something like, "This outcome gives me an opportunity to shine, as I will focus my attention on X, Y, and Z. I accept the challenge of the moment and commit to a positive course of action."

If appropriate, consider thanking the decision-maker for giving you the chance to compete for an opportunity. The way our minds are wired, it's hard to feel gratitude and anger at the same time.

It's okay to take a few minutes to mourn the loss of a great opportunity. Then start to refocus on the things you can control.

GET TO TOMORROW

A natural disaster was the first step in a process that taught me an important lesson in resilience, hope, and commitment. Yes, this chapter is about my experiences.

I didn't set out to have, *Get To Tomorrow,* become a mantra. Over time, as I've shared the phrase, people have said, "Hey, that's pretty good advice. Where did you get it?"

In these moments, I'd mumble something about it being good advice I heard somewhere. For this book, I considered creating a character to convey the idea.

But that would still see me share examples from my professional history and I'm guessing most people don't have a background that includes hurricane relief, TV news, and professional ballet. So I became one of my book's mentors.

Hurricane Relief

Let's get back to the natural disaster or disasters. During a two-year period, my area of Florida was hit by three hurricanes.

Even if you don't suffer injuries or catastrophic damage to your property, these storms are still extremely disruptive in several ways:

1. The power is out and it may not be restored for days or weeks. Meanwhile, it's hot outside and no electricity means no air conditioning.
2. The water that comes from your tap may be contaminated, so you can't drink it.
3. Without power, the food in your refrigerator will soon spoil. Your supply

of non-perishable food may not be as robust as you need.

All these challenges create an immediate need for food, water, and ice. My job was to operate a distribution site that would give people these much-needed supplies. Here's what it involved:

1. The distribution site is created in the empty parking lot of a community college. Normally, the seven-mile drive there wouldn't be too hard. But roughly 12 hours ago, a hurricane passed through the area. This means traffic lights and streetlights are out. Plus, downed trees are blocking roads. Driving to the site is like navigating an obstacle course you've never seen before.

2. At some point, the government issued supplies will arrive in big trucks but you don't know when or how much of the supplies you'll receive. Typically, a set is made up of a case of water, two bags of ice, and a box of non-perishable food.

3. And at some point, volunteers will show up. It could be anywhere from 50 to 100

people. Most of them have never done this kind of work before. In my experience, they ranged in age from 13 to 81. And your volunteers have just lived through an extremely stressful disaster experience and are likely to face hardships in their own homes.

Meanwhile, the site location has been shared by the media and there are cars as far as you can see, lined up, waiting for us to open.

To do this job, you need to be flexible and make a lot of quick decisions. You hope most of them will be good ones.

After a few hours, we had the supplies and enough volunteers to open up one lane of three drive-up stations. Imagine a slightly slower version of a NASCAR pit crew, where the volunteers place the supplies in the car's open trunk. The driver never gets out of the car, as that slows down the process.

On some days, we will eventually open two lanes, with four stations in each lane. If everything goes well, with a good group of volunteers, we can get those eight cars loaded in about 90 seconds.

We'd be doing this, constantly, for at least nine hours a day.

And that's where we get into a *Get To Tomorrow* situation. More on that in just a bit.

The Unfair Challenge

Unfortunately, we did not have an unlimited amount of supplies. On many days, we would run out, either for the rest of the day or until another delivery truck arrived. It's hard to get a status report as many cell phone towers have been damaged.

With that in mind, county leaders decided that every car gets one set of supplies. No exceptions. And we're being monitored by county officials.

For those people who waited for hours and got the supplies, we're heroes. We appreciate their kind words of thanks.

But in some cases, we're also the villains. Because some people chose to carpool to the distribution site. They have IDs that show they live in different places.

We would have to tell them, "Sorry but we're only able to give one set per car."

We did say they could get back in line for another set of supplies but that might see them wait for hours. And there was no guarantee there would still be supplies to give out.

We had to ruin their day. Some even cried out of frustration. Who wants to be a relief worker who can't help someone in need?

But later on that same day, there would be the last dozen or so cars that would get supplies before they ran out. The only reason they got them was due to our following the one set of supplies per car rule. To them, we were heroes.

While this work was meaningful, it was stressful and after a few days you're emotionally spent. And when you're off the job, you're still living with the aftermath of a hurricane. Imagine working a busy and stressful day and then having to drive home in total darkness because there are no streetlights.

By day three, I could tell people were tired, morale was falling, and I needed to deliver a pep talk because sad volunteers tend to disappear.

"Get to tomorrow," I said.

"What does that mean?" people asked.

"We're in a tough situation and it's impossible to please everyone," I said. "But on the whole, we're performing really good work. Let's make sure we focus on that."

I was encouraged by a few nods from the crowd.

"Let's just do our best and make it through the day. It won't be perfect. But every day we get further away from the storm, we'll be closer to our normal lives. But to do that we need to get to tomorrow."

TV News

As an industry, TV news is a perfect fit for *Get To Tomorrow.* Every deadline is fast-approaching, every story is a fight against your competition, and equipment, from cameras to teleprompters, can break at any moment.

It is an exciting and rewarding profession but it can be a roller coaster ride of emotions. Being able to step back, during a stressful day, and say, "Get to tomorrow," is very important for your career and your mental health.

During my news days, I worked as a reporter, a producer, a news anchor, and even a weather anchor. Every job had its challenges and disappointing moments.

Over time, I realized the best news anchors and reporters learned how to navigate these problems. They couldn't prevent things like equipment breaking at the worst possible time.

Rather than panic or let it ruin their day, they kept things in perspective. For instance, the equipment issues were annoying, but those problems could be fixed and tomorrow would be a better day.

They knew you couldn't stop frustrating things from happening. But if you could keep your cool during those moments, you'd maintain your focus and show good leadership to everyone else in the studio. And the viewers might never know something went wrong.

It took me a long time to learn this valuable lesson. There were many times when my competitive side ended up making me feel miserable, after work, on those days when nothing went right.

Professional Ballet

Before I worked in the world of dance, I had heard the phrase, "The show must go on," but little did I know it would become such a big part of my ballet experience.

In this case, the challenges were financial. Sadly, it's the case for many arts groups.

Ballet is a very expensive art form. In our company, we had 11 female dancers. They needed to dance in pointe shoes and those had to be of the highest quality.

The ones we needed to buy sold for roughly $125 a pair. And a dancer could wear out one pair in one rehearsal or one performance.

It wasn't like I could say to the ballerinas, "Could you dance a little less?"

While donations played a major role in our funding, the Great Recession and fallout from the Bernie Madoff Ponzi scheme, limited the money we could raise.

When I started as Executive Director, my goal was to make something good into something great. I soon realized my mission was actually to make sure it could stay open.

I'm proud of the work the staff, board members, donors, and I did to get us through that season. The performances were excellent and the dancing left audiences feeling happy and inspired. Offstage, you'd cut your budget as much as you could but certain costs, like performance venue rentals, couldn't be canceled without a big financial penalty. You'd look to shore up support with current donors and pursue new ones.

Even with all this work, there were days when I would race to the bank to make a critical deposit or payment, moments before it would be too late. I even cold-called a total stranger, in another part of the country, who had a reputation for supporting struggling arts groups.

While there were daily victories (the cold call produced a $500 gift), every one seemed to come with two new challenges.

Soon, you're working longer and longer hours because there's always one more problem you need to solve. Meanwhile, the pressure continues to rise.

I realized this was a classic, *Get To Tomorrow* moment. While our challenges were considerable, there was no magic wand that could solve everything at once.

Instead, the focus needed to be on daily progress. Could we end the day a little better in some areas? Was there some kind of victory or achievement that showed we were making progress, even if it was incremental?

This mindset gives you some breathing room during tough times. And there were times when nothing went right or maybe things got a little worse. I realized that day's victory was simply making it through the day.

Get To Tomorrow in Everyday Life

There's a good chance you're not fighting hurricanes, racing to cover the day's news, or trying to keep a ballet company afloat. But I'm guessing, in today's world, you're dealing with some everyday challenges. Some that come to mind include:

- Identity theft

- Healthcare costs

- Government bureaucracy

- Inflation

None of these challenges come with quick solutions. In fact, most seem to take more time than they should, involve countless phone prompts, and feature confusing terms and conditions.

Worse yet, in the end you're often left with few solutions and more questions. And that feeling of helplessness tends to keep you up at night.

One time, I was sharing with my father the pain that came with having to deal with a government agency.

"I know I'm right. I have documentation to prove it. I've shared that documentation several times. And yet my problem has not been solved," I complained.

"It sounds like a carnival game," my father said.

Suddenly, everything made sense. While it's possible to win a carnival game, the operators do some sneaky things that make it harder than you think. In this situation, the carnival holds the upper hand, and there's not much you can do about it.

How does this fit into a *Get To Tomorrow* philosophy?

There will be days when you just have to give your very best effort toward these annoying situations and then see how they turn out. While you may be 100% correct in your way of seeing the situation, there's no guarantee things will turn out your way. Reality may not match your expectations.

You're battling ineffective bureaucratic systems that are sometimes rigged against you. It's like playing a carnival game. Emotionally detach yourself from the outcome.

Do what it takes to get through the process and then give yourself a pat on the back for the effort. Let go of the frustration and anxiety and move on to a new day.

Otherwise, the angst that comes from an ineffective system will stay with you or grow. Better to make it through the tough day and then turn your attention elsewhere.

Big Picture Takeaways

Life comes with challenges and sometimes they involve unfair or no-win situations.

Your ability to navigate these challenges and keep them in perspective will help define your success.

Don't get hung up on outcomes, when you have very little control of the situation. Your control is about how you handle your reaction. And yes, this takes some practice.

Action Steps

Realize when you are in a *Get To Tomorrow* situation. Then refocus your expectations and effort.

This is the kind of thing that is not taught in

school. It's not a bad idea to discuss these situations with your kids or professionals who are early in their careers. It can prevent a lot of frustration down the road.

In the rear-view mirror of life, our problems will likely appear smaller than you thought.

BEAUTIFUL IS HARD

How far do we stretch ourselves when we're already uncomfortable? I thought about this question when I was watching a ballet class.

The students were a small group of dancers known as trainees. These performers, who typically range in age from 16 to 21, are promising dancers but they're not quite at the level where they can be members of a professional dance company.

As an outsider to the world of dance, I wanted to learn more about this program, which could be described as similar to an internship or an apprenticeship.

The trainees play an important role in a dance company, as they're able to take on small roles in big productions, where there are more parts than professional company dancers. They also get to attend daily classes with the professional members and have exposure to top choreographers.

While our trainees were paid a small weekly stipend, most were more excited to receive the world-class training that could take them to a new level in their careers.

"Let's start from first position," Melinda, the instructor, tells the group. The trainees move as one as they gracefully enter the stance.

As the class continues, the moves become more complex and well beyond anything I could ever attempt. I start to feel self-conscious, as I realize I'm slumping in my chair.

This was especially true because everyone in this class is demonstrating near-perfect posture. Ballet is a very technical art form and one that builds on the basics. You must have excellent form and technique.

The instructor will occasionally stop the class to correct a dancer's form. An arm or a leg may need to be bent a certain way. This even involves where your eyes are looking.

"Cassandra, I know that you want to bring your right leg forward but it needs to go back," Melinda said.

This kind of physical dedication to the details is a big part of the life of a dancer.

"Over time you will develop muscle memory but you've got to train your body to do it the right way," Melinda said.

When done correctly, the moves appear effortless. But I know, in reality, they demand an incredible amount of body control and concentration.

"Keep working," Melinda said in encouragement. "Beautiful is hard."

Those three words mean everything to a dancer.

Try This at Home

I realize it's not easy to read about movement in dance, especially if you're not familiar with ballet. Allow me to share a more relatable example.

Imagine you need to pick up a 20 pound box off the floor. You need to show the correct form, so you lift with your knees and not your back. You also need to make the movement look smooth and artistic.

While holding the box at your waist, turn 90 degrees to the left and then slowly lift the box over your head. Then bring the box down to your waist and rotate back to your original position. Finally, put the box back on the ground.

Imagine doing this several times and each time it needs to be done perfectly. And think that's just one move of many.

Learning to Love Uncomfortable

Beautiful Is Hard represents a commitment to excellence. When a dancer starts to get tired, I'm sure it's tempting to cut corners on a move or pursue a shortcut and hope no one notices.

However, the nature of ballet demands perfection. You have to follow the basic moves. The opportunity for self-expression comes later.

And the training never ends. Every day, the entire dance company takes part in at least an hour-long class that is designed to prepare the body and mind for that day's work.

I have no idea if any of the trainees I saw that day went on to professional careers. But I do know if they embrace *Beautiful Is Hard,* then they'll enjoy success in life.

Many retired dancers excel in second careers, even in fields unrelated to dance. I think their success is rooted in those countless hours spent chasing perfection.

Big Picture Takeaways

When *Beautiful is Hard,* success becomes easier but you have to work for it. It represents a commitment to yourself.

The excitement of pursuing something we love, can override our fear of the uncomfortable.

Consider the level of your skills. You could be the best dancer in your local community but below average on a statewide level. Where is your focus?

What daily actions do you need to take to maintain a strong commitment to ongoing professional success?

Action Steps

Are there moments when you or others cut corners or take shortcuts in time-honored processes? Have people, like an instructor or coach, who will hold you accountable.

Someone who is really good at this helps you

re-wire your brain and hear that accountability voice, even when that person is not around.

When it comes to self-improvement, get specific. Vague promises are easy to undermine.

When you've worked hard and accomplished something, give yourself some kind of reward. It can be very tempting to climb one mountain and then immediately move to the next one. Take some time to enjoy the view.

One day, without thinking, you'll be able to perform something that once was incredibly hard for you.

DON'T OPEN THE OVEN

A news investigation into a kitchen gadget taught me a valuable lesson in professional confidence and how to be a good supervisor. At the time, I was reporting on a weekly segment called, *Does It Work Wednesday?*

Every week, we would test a different household gadget (the kind you might see featured in infomercials) with the help of someone who worked in that field.

On this day, I'm in a restaurant kitchen with a chef, and he's helping me evaluate a mixing bowl that features a built-in mixing mechanism. The device was advertised as an easier way to perform the everyday task.

The chef's name was Charlie and he thought the mixer did an okay job of combining the ingredients from the cake mix we supplied. He thought amateur bakers or people with arthritis might enjoy the product.

But this is not the story of a gadget. Instead, it's about what happened when we finished recording the segment.

"Gentlemen, we have a bowl full of cake batter. We might as well bake it," Chef Charlie said.

News crews never turn down free food and especially cake, so we were happy to wait and chat with Charlie. Before long, the smell of a double chocolate cake filled the air.

It was noticed by a member of the kitchen staff who was prepping that day's meals. Out of curiosity, he started reaching toward the oven handle when he received a warning.

"Don't open the oven," Charlie playfully

yelled at him. "Give me five more minutes and then the oven is all yours."

The employee grinned and said, "Yes, Chef! Trust the recipe."

Charlie nodded in encouragement at the employee, turned to us and said, "In the kitchen, sometimes you have to unlearn some bad habits. This is especially true with people who open the oven too early."

"Why would that be a problem?" I asked.

"Opening the oven lets out a lot of the beautiful hot air inside. Cold air then replaces it," Charlie said. "That affects the cooking process in a big way and may create uneven baking."

"What should you do if you're not sure if the recipe time is correct?" I asked.

"If you need to take a look at how things are baking, you could use the oven window and the interior light," Charlie said. "But even then, you can't see below the surface. You need to have confidence in your recipe and not interrupt the baking process."

I have to admit, I was suddenly more interested in baking tips, than I was in the effectiveness of the mixing gadget.

"Sometimes, I may open the oven a few times," I said. "I'm guessing that's really bad."

"It is. You're undermining the oven because it can't do its job," he said. "Someone spent a lot of time creating a recipe. It's been tested in many situations. Confident chefs trust the recipe, at least for the first time. Otherwise, you won't know if it really works."

A Familiar Taste

A few minutes later, we're enjoying the cake. I realize *Don't Open the Oven* has a meaning that goes beyond the kitchen.

"I've had some supervisors who were micromanagers," I said. "It sounds like they're *opening the oven* and not trusting their employees to do their jobs."

"I need to see everything that's happening in this kitchen," Charlie says with a dramatic wave. "But while I see my team doing their jobs, I don't closely watch them executing their jobs. I'm not looking over their shoulders. If I've hired someone who is good and trained them in how I want things done, then I don't need to watch them."

"What if there are mistakes?" I asked.

"Mistakes will happen in a kitchen. I ask myself if the mistake is correctable. If someone can't do the job, then I'm going to make a change," Charlie said. "But with our hiring and training processes, we're going to know if you're good or not."

He then pointed across the room at the dishwasher. "We buy a good, industrial dishwasher that allows us to never run out of plates and silverware. Once I see it works, then I don't watch it doing its job. That would be a waste of time. My focus needs to be on making great food."

Big Picture Takeaways

Not feeling confident about a process can lead to our undermining that process.

When employees don't seem to be doing something correctly, revisit your training. In some instances, it's better to retrain everyone at once, rather than spend your day offering constant corrections.

Sometimes the best advice comes when you least expect it. In covering this story, I thought all I was going to learn about was the usefulness of a kitchen gadget. Instead, I got a high level business lesson.

Action Steps

Take a week or two and track if certain repeated employee problems are taking up too much of your time. Try to find a solution that fixes the problem and keeps you out of a babysitter role.

Sometimes, employees will drift into shortcuts or lazy behaviors that affect your processes. You may want to enlist employees to self-correct the problem.

You could say something like, "Everyone, it looks like there has been some cutting of corners lately. You know the way we want things done and why we need them done that way. Can you clean up this problem on your own?"

Some of the best supervisors make you feel like they're always around to support you, even if they are not nearby.

WATCH YOURSELF WILLIE

A mixture of terror and excitement filled the conference room at the TV station. At the time, my colleagues and I were meeting with a news anchor coach.

In an industry that is full of consultants, who provide little guidance beyond repeating certain catchphrases, Willie was the real deal. During his career, he led several successful news organizations and shaped the careers of many talented reporters and anchors.

While he was in the room as a favor to a colleague, you could tell he was genuinely interested in giving us some guidance.

You want to hear that you're brilliant but realize you probably have room to improve. The fast-paced nature of news makes it hard to get much feedback, other than someone saying, "Good story."

We knew the feedback Willie would provide would be at a much higher level, based on years of success. It would be truthful, constructive, and priceless.

During the session, Willie watched a replay of a newscast with us. Between segments and stories, he'd stop the playback and then comment on how we were performing.

This was a time to check your ego at the door. Willie's advice could provide a path for you to make changes that could help you get a job at a larger station. This usually comes with a bigger paycheck, a better news operation, and more opportunities to grow your career.

At the end of the session, Willie gave us one more suggestion.

"Tonight, I'm just looking at one newscast and there's only so much I can learn from it," he said. "After every newscast, I want you to watch yourself and evaluate your performance."

"What should we look for?" one of my colleagues asked.

"Find those moments when you did something well and really connected with the story and the viewer," he responded. "You want to figure out what you did and how you can do that thing more often. Sometimes it's just about reacting to the story you're reading and not just reading it like a shopping list."

There were a few surprised looks and groans.

"I understand," Willie said. "No one likes watching themselves. But it's how you get better. Otherwise, you're guessing about how you should improve."

Everyone in the room understood that last point. While anchoring a newscast, you don't get any audience feedback because you're just looking into a camera. You have to imagine and assume your audience likes or even loves you.

"Once I worked with Dean, who was a longtime anchor, at a popular TV station," Willie said. "He was tired of being a big fish in a little pond. Dean wanted to move up to a larger station but could never get that next big job."

"Did he watch himself?" I asked.

"He did not and he made fun of his female co-anchors who did," he said. "But then I pointed out to Dean that two of those ladies were now working in larger markets because they spent roughly 15 minutes a day, seeing how they could improve."

Suddenly, Willie's advice sounded a lot more attractive!

Big Picture Takeaways

Your ability to be open to feedback can give you an edge in your career. As I find myself in the world of professional speaking, another profession where people don't like to watch themselves, I still follow Willie's advice.

Whenever I take to the stage, I either record the audio of my keynote session or set up a small camera in the audience to capture video. I do this for two reasons:

1. During a talk, in the moment, I may say something brilliant that I've never thought of before. With a recording, there's no chance of my forgetting what I said.

2. Even a seasoned presentation gets better through little adjustments. A pause or saying a line in a slightly different way, can get a much better reaction from the audience. You can't make those changes if you don't know where you are.

There are times when I watch my talks and agonize over any little mistake. Every stumble is like a knife to your ego. I think that's a common feeling for speakers, as well as perfectionists in general.

But in those sessions, I also discover golden

nuggets, when a small change goes exceptionally well. Or you handle a distraction, like plates accidentally breaking on the floor, in a fun way that relates to your talk. You don't get these priceless moments or just the chance to improve, unless you summon the courage and watch yourself.

Action Steps

Create a defined process for how you and others will get better. Is it easily followed and repeatable? Notice, I did not ask if it's fun. Sometimes improvement involves a little pain.

Make sure annual reviews include clear next steps. Don't let these sessions become glorified coffee breaks, where shortcomings are only discussed in casual terms.

When evaluating someone, don't just focus on what went wrong. You should also build on strengths.

Courage is often the price of admission for growth and progress.

DON'T BE AFRAID

What if three words could deliver artistic courage to people who are already among the best in the business at what they do? I saw it happen at an open rehearsal for a symphony orchestra.

The symphony is just a day away from its first performance of a piece that's been around for decades but is new to the orchestra. I'm sitting in the audience, getting a behind-the-scenes look at how the conductor, Carlos, makes his final adjustments.

While the score contains all the musical

notes, it's up to the conductor to interpret the piece. Carlos will likely put his own spin on how it is played.

Through research and experience, a conductor makes decisions on things like the speed the music is played or how loud certain instruments should sound. Despite what cartoons may suggest, the job is not just about waving your arms.

Keep in mind the conductor is the only one who has the full score. The players just have the parts for their instruments. They rely on Carlos to have the big picture in mind.

To my ears, the rehearsal is going well but Carlos will periodically stop the music and ask for some adjustments.

The tone of these corrections is positive. There's no need for yelling, as everyone is highly skilled in their roles. But they need to embrace adjustments. Sometimes, that is easier said than done.

There was one section the orchestra worked

on repeatedly. It was obvious the sound in the conductor's mind was not the one he was hearing. Eventually, Carlos addressed the entire orchestra with a simple message for the piece.

"Don't be afraid," he said playfully.

This comment generated a few nods and laughs. It also broke the tension, in what could be a frustrating situation for a stage full of high performers.

Perhaps this was permission for the orchestra members to go outside their comfort zones and try something new.

A couple of days later, I was in the audience for the performance. The orchestra earns its reputation for excellence.

Not surprisingly, there were a few standing ovations. During these moments, when the instruments are lowered, you can see the pleasure of playing shown on the faces of the orchestra. It's not just about the applause but being able to perform well at something you love.

Big Picture Takeaways

It's easy to give out orders but harder to give instructions that will inspire change. Sometimes people need permission to do something different.

Most top performers want to be coached. They didn't get where they are without others helping them. Constant praise is a small meal, of empty calories, for the mind.

The conductor is the leader of the orchestra and must have a clear vision of what he or she wants. If people can tell you've done your homework, then they're more likely to follow you. Otherwise, you're just a random person, waving a baton.

In leadership, you can debate issues and change your opinion, but you need to ultimately have one communicated vision of what you want. It's okay to replace the old way with the new but make sure you explain why the change is necessary.

Finally, Carlos used a playful tone as a way to ask the orchestra members to get out of their comfort zones. Had he delivered the request with too much intensity, then people may have tightened up and resisted change.

Action Steps

If you need to deliver a pep talk at work, boil down your message into a few words, like, "Don't be afraid."

You may have detailed instructions to convey but build them around that memorable phrase. Some prefer to use an acronym in these situations.

When your organization receives the equivalent of a standing ovation, make sure you share the praise with the members of your *orchestra*. Sometimes it's strategically smart to share some of the limelight with those who have room to grow.

When asking for or demanding change, remember that while you may be talking to one person, others may be watching and judging your performance. Take the time to consider how your remarks could impact the workplace culture.

When you hire people who are good at what they do, change can happen much faster and much smoother.

THE UNINSPIRING EXAMPLES

Let's begin with a disclaimer. If someone else was writing this book, then there's a good chance I might be featured in this chapter.

Over the years, I've probably done a thing or two that others may have considered examples of what not to do. I'm far from perfect.

I believe we all have opportunities for growth and the chance to make better decisions in the future. Sometimes, hearing a story of when someone didn't perform well, gives us much needed inspiration to take steps to improve ourselves.

In this book I've featured inspiring people and lessons I've learned along the way. My eyes were also open to those who left me uninspired and disappointed.

It's funny but they are often the ones who are remembered most. Unfortunately, it's for all the wrong reasons.

The Escape Artist

Barry is the recently hired CEO of a successful nonprofit. The organization could be described by employees as being a touchy-feely place. Barry is not a touchy-feely person.

In order to get to his office, on the second floor of the building, he has to walk past the reception desk and either take the stairs or an elevator. During that short trip, Barry is likely to encounter at least one or two employees who say, "Good morning," or engage in some kind of small talk.

Barry hates small talk and interacting with staff. Maybe he was an extreme introvert but he wasn't even willing to fake a friendly conversation.

Before long, he makes what he feels is a game-changing discovery. There is a fire exit that will allow him to enter and exit the building, unseen.

This solution requires him to walk around the building, step through mud, and climb over a bush to get to his secret entrance. But apparently, these actions were preferable to talking to his employees.

As you might guess, Barry was not a good fit for his nonprofit's workplace culture. Eventually, for many reasons, there was a parting of the ways.

I understand that some people may be introverts and feel drained by casual conversations. But trying to hide from the problem is not addressing the problem.

Especially if you are in a leadership role, be transparent about your strengths and weaknesses. It allows people the chance to adjust to your working style.

Otherwise, you're allowing what could be a minor quirk to grow, like a weed, into a major issue.

Hiding from a problem does not eliminate the problem. It puts a spotlight on it.

Nickel and Dime Danny

It's not uncommon to have a job where you feel like you're underpaid. In most cases, you look to move on. For Danny, it was about trying to get revenge against his employer.

Danny worked as a studio camera operator at a TV station. By the time we were colleagues, he had been there for a couple of years.

Danny was good at his job but always complained about how management treated him. Granted, the station was little cheap but that tends to be the industry rule, rather than the exception. I never saw him being treated worse than anyone else.

While working together on the morning show, I noticed that Danny would show up looking like he had just rolled out of bed. I found out he actually was doing this.

On morning shows that start airing at 5 a.m., it's not unusual for people to start work hours earlier. You'd see the studio crew and producers wearing a lot of sweatshirts and baseball caps. It makes sense, as getting an extra 15 to 20 minutes of sleep is more important than being dressed to impress.

Danny took this to a new level. Anything most people would do at home, to get ready for work, he did on the job. Getting dressed, brushing his teeth, shaving, and bathroom time were all things he took care of while on the clock.

"For as little as they pay me, they can pay me to get ready. I do as little as possible at home," he said with pride.

Over time, the morning crew got used to

Danny's routine. Upper management was likely fast asleep and unaware of his protest.

In the big picture, this was a case of mismatched energy and outrage. Some jobs aren't the best paid or respected. In these cases, learn what you can and then find a better position.

Even if Danny had live-streamed his morning ritual to station management, I doubt they would have cared. They just needed a warm body to operate the studio camera.

Inspired by a popular philosophical question, let me ask, "If a protest isn't noticed, did it really happen?"

Chronic complaining rarely produces change.

Easy Hike Earl

Earl loved being in nature and he found his perfect job as a wilderness guide. He also had an extremely short tenure doing that same job at a nearby resort.

At conferences and retreats, it's not unusual to have an afternoon blocked off for a fun activity. It might be golf, fishing, or karaoke. Attendees and their families can take part in the fun.

At this event, organizers wanted to do something outdoors, as the resort was in a beautiful part of the country. They asked the resort team to find a guide who could take them on an engaging hike.

The resort staff reached out to Earl and he was excited to introduce the group to the wildlife, flowers, and scenic views that make the area so special. This seemed like a perfect match.

"It was a disaster," resort staff told me. "People said it was more like a forced march."

I found out that while Earl knew everything about nature, he didn't know anything about the group. He set up what he called "an easy hike" on a nearby trail.

It turns out Earl's definition of easy and the group's understanding differed significantly. He set up a challenging five-mile hike, which required climbing over large rocks and holding onto ropes, bolted to the sides of cliffs.

Keep in mind, that for some of the attendees, the walk from their rooms to the conference center was more like their definition of an easy hike.

"We had a lot of complaints," the resort staffer admitted. "We never used Earl again. And I don't think he enjoyed the conference crowd."

Earl planned an outdoor experience that the members of his hiking community would have loved. The effort was there. The understanding was not.

It's sad because had he just scaled back his plans, he might have been one of the most memorable parts of the conference, as well as created some new lifelong hikers.

You can be an expert at something but the

people you're working with may be much less experienced in that area. You have to meet them where they are.

The *Easy Hike Earl* situation, is a common challenge for a lot of businesses. One of the biggest complaints I hear about large companies is that upper management does not understand what things are like on the ground floor. Talented people with one set of skills are making really big decisions for those with other talents.

This challenge was turned into the popular TV show, *Undercover Boss*, where leaders put on disguises and performed the duties of regular employees at their own companies. Usually, this perspective gave them valuable insights and sometimes led to changes in day-to-day operations.

To prevent the *Easy Hike Earl* problem, you don't have to create a reality TV show. But take some time to do research on your audience, otherwise known as your employees.

You may need to push people but do not create unreasonable and unachievable demands. That will cause them to check out and start looking for jobs elsewhere.

Instead, have some honest conversations and agree to a level of expectations.

A surprising number of our problems are rooted in assumptions.

ABOUT THE AUTHOR

For meeting professionals, Ken Okel is a trusted partner, as he delivers actionable, engaging, and memorable programs. He understands the need to perform at a high level on the job, when the pressure is on, having worked in broadcast news, hurricane relief, and professional ballet (not a typo).

These highly competitive and pressure-packed professions taught Ken priceless insider knowledge, which he shares with audiences as an in-demand motivational keynote speaker.

Other professional adventures have seen him write the book, *Stuck on Yellow*, host the weekly podcast, *The 2 Minute Takeaway*, and promote everything from global brands to a three-legged kitten.

As a child, Ken loved playing with Lego and letting his imagination run wild. Today, he flexes those creative muscles with meeting planners, as they collaborate on his presentations.

On stage, you might see Ken make a point, with ballet, about trust at work. Yes, Ken breaks out some dance moves!

Or he quickly changes clothes (offstage), as part of a story about dealing with unexpected change, during an *airport fashion emergency.*

And he might inspire you to approach challenges differently, with the takeaways of a *police dog attack,* when Ken was wearing a padded suit.

This award-winning journalist continues to use his broadcasting skills, leading panels, and on-stage interviews, serving as an Emcee, and appearing (slightly taller) in virtual talks. He also creates special preview videos to help clients market and promote their events.

Ken is a Past President and a two-time *Member of the Year* of the Florida Speakers Association and a 20-year member of the National Speakers Association.

When he's not speaking, Ken may be looking at his Fitbit, as he chases his daily goal of 20,000 steps. After he sits down, he may be online with members of his family, who live in France, South Korea, and across the United States. Ken is proud to call South Florida home.

To learn more about Ken and see him on stage, visit www.KenOkel.com

BULK ORDERS OF THIS BOOK

You can order bulk copies of this book and Ken's other book, *Stuck On Yellow*. Bulk orders start at 10 copies.

For more information or to start the process, email TVGuy@KenOkel.com and put "Book Bulk Order" in the subject line.